Tiny Houses

The Ultimate Beginner's Guide!

By James Clark

Table of Contents

Introduction

This book contains proven steps and strategies on how to get started with your dream tiny home. Living tiny is an entire movement designed to make homes affordable and people more mobile, without losing all the accouterments they desire.

The average size of a new house, built in the United States, is 2,400 square feet. In the last few decades, the size of homes has increased, taking up large carbon footprints. This has also led to an increase in maintenance and energy costs. If everyone in the world lived in such a house, it would be impossible to keep up with oil and propane production.

A recent U.S. census, done on home sizes and cost, show that the average cost for a new home is $360,000. Most homeowners have to take out a 30-year mortgage to cover the cost of their home. It usually means debt for years.

The tiny house movement brings has the potential to bring people back to financial stability. It is a way for young college graduates to buy their first home and not throw money away renting. Tiny houses are also designed with a smaller carbon footprint, low energy costs, and innovation to make living comfortable and exciting.

The tiny house movement philosophy is about living a minimalist lifestyle that is eco-friendly, affordable and that brings people back to the important things in life. Most tiny house owners are able to gain more savings than traditional homeowners because of the low-cost investment.

You can join the tiny house movement, too, by making a decision to live affordably and with luxury. Tiny house owners choose between two options when they go tiny: mobile or stationary. What you need is an architect, or someone experienced building tiny houses, to help you with the engineering of your tiny house, an idea, and the desire to see it come to life.

Start your tiny house living and discover what your home could truly offer you. This potentially includes financial freedom and the ability to travel, so don't wait. Now is the time to start planning and find out if you can truly go tiny.

Chapter 1

What is a Tiny House?

A tiny house is a regular home that has been shrunken down to an affordable living space for anyone who doesn't need big spaces, or–a mortgage.

Tiny houses are built in one of two ways: mobile or stationary. A mobile tiny house is built on a trailer specifically designed or enhanced to carry the load of the house. A static, or stationary, tiny home is built on a plot of land, to give you permanence.

Mobile Tiny Houses

Mobile tiny houses offer a variety of benefits:

- They allow you to travel while offering you a place to live.
- You have to build according to the dimensions of the trailer, which enables better planning.
- You're limited in size which helps keep the costs down.
- You can be very innovative with your mobile tiny house design.

Stationary Tiny Houses

Stationary tiny houses also provide several benefits:

- You don't have to worry about pulling a trailer.
- You can choose a plot of land you like, invest in the property, and the tiny home, providing more equity.

- If you wish to add more space to your tiny house, you have that option.

Whether you choose a mobile or static tiny home, you know there are benefits for you to enjoy and you have the luxury of being very creative in making a small space fit your lifestyle.

The average size, for stationary tiny houses, ranges from 96 square feet to 1,000 square feet. There are some, in the tiny house community who firmly believe that only houses under 220 square feet can be considered a tiny house. Yet, 1,000 square feet is considered tiny compared to the average home size of 2,400 square feet.

Mobile tiny houses are going to be smaller than static tiny houses, in terms of average size ranges. There are only so many square feet you can put on a trailer when the dimensions have to fit the trailer. As a result, tiny house builders have become extremely creative, and mobile tiny houses, in particular, have pushed the limits on tiny house height.

Many people use flatbed trailers to build tiny houses. Typical trailers can reach up to 53 feet in length and are 8 feet & 6 inches wide. There are also different types of trailers, such as those with a neck that will take away some of the flat building space. The drop deck style is popular among tiny house owners for the storage it can provide underneath the neck, plus the upper area for a bedroom.

Mobile tiny homes have a limit on how high they can be built. The house has to be able to clear under underpasses and bridges, which means 13 feet is about the maximum height. However, there have been some very inventive tiny home designers that have figured out a way to beat the 13-foot limitation. With systems such as pulleys and winches, there are moveable roofs that lift up when the tiny house is parked. Other individuals have created more width in the tiny home by building side extensions (like camper RVs). When parked, the sides are pushed out and when mobile they are pushed in.

Your tiny home can be built to your specifications and within engineering parameters. You can decide on the desired floor plan and determine how much space you truly need. Your preference of mobility will also impact the floor plan you choose.

Chapter 2

Why the Tiny House Movement?

There are multiple reasons why people choose to join the tiny house movement. People want more financial stability, to escape the rat race, to have a second home, to enjoy the outdoors, or to lower their carbon footprint. Sometimes it is all of these reasons and for some, it is a combination of them. Each person is different. One young lady built her tiny home because she is a traveling nurse, going where she's most needed around the USA. Another person wanted the freedom to travel the lower 48 while working freelance jobs, but also to afford a home one day.

Below are the top reasons why people choose to live or own a tiny house.

Reason 1: Financial

Financial motivations are extremely high on most people's list when choosing tiny houses over traditional homes. There are numerous US residents who know they can't afford a regular home and a mortgage, but they can afford a tiny house.

Traditional homes can be found for $75,000 and upwards of several million. The average is $360,000 in recent years. Homes that are low cost usually require a lot of renovation or are not in the greatest neighborhoods. Over time, one could spend more than the average price of a home just by renovating a home they bought for $75,000.

The initial expenses of owning a large traditional home are not only expensive and require a mortgage, but there are also maintenance costs to consider. Maintaining a larger home requires more financial backing and energy. Maintenance, electricity, gas, and cleaning are all downsides to a regular sized home. The expense of cleaning one's house is either your time and energy or hiring someone to do it.

Tiny House Financial Benefits

- Less than 400 square feet for most mobile homes equals lower energy costs.

- Fewer square feet means less energy expenditure on cleaning. There is no need for a cleaning staff.

- Maintenance is less costly because there is less square footage to re-roof, re-sizing, or re-paint.

Most tiny house owners see a significant decrease in their energy consumption and bills. You can typically expect a 37 percent reduction in energy costs for a stationary tiny home, without solar panels. Owners who add solar panels to their tiny homes tend to see a greater decrease in energy costs. It's been reported that solar panels, on tiny house roofs, can yield up to a 75 % reduction in energy costs and in many cases 100% reduction because all the energy is able to come from the solar panels.

Reason 2: Return on Investment

One of the biggest arguments most standard homeowners have, is how can you gain a return on your investment with a tiny house? If your family becomes larger or you have the funds to live in a larger house, how are you going to get any money back from the tiny house you built? Is there even any equity in a tiny house?

Well, depending on how you construct your tiny house there can be value in it. A mobile tiny house is going to be more like an RV. In fact, you have to have RV insurance on your mobile tiny house trailer. Since it is not a manufactured home, but a livable house like an RV, it will be valued more like a vehicle or an RV than a house.

If you build a stationary tiny house, then you have the equity and property taxes. You can also get a traditional mortgage if you need to, in order to finance the build. The return on investment is going to differ between stationary and mobile.

For mobile tiny homes, your choice to rent it out or sell it when you are ready for something larger is going to depend on the market. Where you intend to park (station) your mobile tiny house usually determines how much you can charge to rent. You can also rent your tiny house to customers who want to take the home on the road. The renting costs are at the owner's digression and are usually measured by the amount of time the customer wants to have it. Owners can thus charge daily, weekly, monthly or for yearly use.

The other option is selling your tiny house. Tiny homeowners sell their homes if they want a quick return on their investment. The downside is that you have equipped it for your needs and wants. Selling it to a new person is not as easy because the potential buyer needs something that will truly work for their lifestyle and not yours. People have had success selling their tiny houses for 25 to 100 percent of the costs they put into the home. In other words, like a car, RV, or another mobile vehicle, you tend to lose money on the resale.

If you go with one of the more popular versions, such as a Tumbleweed mobile home with only minor modifications to the blueprints, then you have a higher chance of breaking even on the purchase.

Stationary tiny homes offer a better return on your investment. For one, property values increase. Two, you can rent out your tiny home to visitors. Tiny House shows reveal you can get anywhere from $100 to $400 per week for a tiny house rental depending on where you live. Florida tiny homes, for rent, can be more than $400 a week if they are near Miami, the Keys, or Orlando.

If you park your mobile home in an RV park, permanently, for the rental season, such as snowbirds, you can expect to make at least the same per week.

There are also tiny home rentals per night. You can be earning anywhere from $100 to $400 per night, depending on your tiny home's fame, and where it is located. Most people doing weekly or monthly rentals are going to discount the amount being charged to make it a favorable situation for the renters.

As an example, The Cottage at the Winchester Manor in New Market, Alabama is a 100-year-old cottage that was renovated. It rents for $100 per night. The Hobbit Cabin in Talkeetna, Alaska rents for $135 per night. All small homes. There are definitely ways you can get your return on your investment by renting.

Just remember, if you are going to start renting your tiny house, you need to look at the market you live in, whether you have a mobile or stationary house. Sometimes you can charge more than a night in a hotel because the home has a kitchen with more amenities than a hotel room. But, above all people want to experience living in a tiny house.

Reason 3: Taxes and Insurance

Property taxes for a stationary mobile home give you a financial break. Property taxes are based on the land and home. The larger the home, the more you pay in taxes. It is always dependent on the city and state where you live, but in general, smaller homes are going to have a lower property tax.

Insurance is where things become interesting. For starters, you are going to save on insurance with a tiny home, whether you are paying RV insurance or homeowners insurance. Homeowners insurance premiums are based on the size of your home. The smaller your home, the less value your home has for a rebuild. In the insurance world, homeowner's insurance covers the exterior as well as the goods you have within.

Mobile tiny homes are different. For mobile tiny homes, you are not going to have property taxes, unless you buy land to park your tiny home on. However, you can have RV insurance on these homes. They are considered a trailer in the insurance world, like an RV trailer. You will need to shop around and determine the best value. Not all RV insurance companies work the same. There are some that may not be able to cover the valuable items you are traveling with. In this regard, you may need homeowners and RV insurance. If you need both, it is still less than owning 2,400 square feet or more. But this also needs to be qualified. The savings you have on insurance are dependent on the company, your credit scores, and if you are bundling insurance products. If you have bad credit or choose the wrong company, you could be paying the same amount in insurance as you paid for your regular sized home or apartment rental.

Reason 4: Escaping the Rat Race Early

Besides the financial motivations, some people are looking to escape from the nine to five lifestyle earlier than most people with a mortgage. You have the option of retiring earlier and traveling more when you have fewer costs weighing you down.

If you have insurance expenses, groceries, and little electricity costs, and only parking fees, you could be saving nearly $3,000 per month towards retirement and travel. The odds of retiring early and in comfort are looking better right? Of course, they are, which is why the tiny house movement continues to grow.

Reason 5: Summer/Vacation Mobile Homes

Some people want to be able to travel more, without leaving their home behind. Having a second home that is tiny and mobile fits their needs. Traveling with a mobile tiny house geometrically adds to the excitement of traveling.

A mobile tiny house also gives people the luxury of escaping bad weather seasons. For instance, you might live in Florida. In the summer months, it is hot and oppressive. With a mobile tiny house, you could travel up to New England, see the west, and find cool places to be, when temperatures in Florida reach 100 degrees Fahrenheit. If you live along the coast, you could travel inland during hurricane season. For those who live with snow and blizzards, you can travel south.

Another great reason for choosing tiny houses is because you get to live in the outdoors. Most of the tiny house community loves the outdoors and being one with nature. They want to be in nature and not in their home. They design their home to bring nature in by leaving open giant lanai doors in their tiny homes.

Reason 6: Carbon Footprint

Living in a tiny house, you have the option of using all energy efficient appliances, toilets, and showers. Solar panels, rainwater collection, and combustible toilets ensure you can live for the environment. Incinerating toilets are friendly because they do not use water. Instead, after each use, you burn your waste. Composting toilets are another option, where your waste is turned into odorless compost that can be reused for plants and fertilizing the earth.

Depending on the weather, with rainwater collection systems, you won't need to fill up with water at every RV stop you make. You can be collecting it as you park or drive somewhere. It does need to be filtered, but this may be a better option than using the chemical city water you are probably using now.

Chapter 3

Engineering a Tiny House

Tiny house plans can be found all over the internet. However, most people have specific needs and desires. You want your home to fit your style and needs, thus, you have some decisions to make. Engineering a tiny house is going to take into account various areas of design in order to construct the tiny house of your dreams.

Identify the Constraints for your Tiny House

Your budget is one of the constraints you will face for a tiny house. You should have an idea of what you have in the bank, what you are willing to spend, and now you need to decide how you can get what you want for that budget.

There are two ways to build a tiny house: hiring a professional or doing the work on your own. If you plan to build your own tiny house, you need the proper experience. If you have never built a home, let alone held a construction tool, then you need to hire the work done. It will take more of your budget to hire the labor, but only when you look at the black and white numbers. Imagine if you knew nothing about building a house, made cuts wrong, spent twice or three times the hours building it as projected, and then you realize, why it actually costs you less to hire a professional.

Other constraints are going to be whether you design your own tiny house, or if you hire someone to create the plans and the architecture of your tiny house. Again, you may need to hire a professional to ensure you are within the proper building codes for your state.

Your tiny house foundation will determine other build constraints. A tiny mobile house will have constraints on the width, length, and height based on the trailer you purchase.

Trailer Size

The trailer size is going to help you determine the design you draw or have drawn up. If you already know the size you want your home to be, then you will need to get a trailer that fits the size.

When it comes to buying a trailer, like most things, you can buy used or new. There is a caution against buying used unless you know the dealer or the history of the trailer. Trailers like most anything can become derelict over time. If someone constantly kept their used trailer outside in the rain and it rusted then you could be looking at more expense to repair it. It is often safer to buy a new trailer to ensure its reliability.

Hiring an engineer or architect is also good if you are going to build a mobile tiny house because there are weight constraints to consider. Trailers need to handle the weight of the load. You would need to figure out the design and determine the weight of that design when empty and when filled with all your possessions. You may need to add an extra axle or support for the home, which determines the amount you are going to spend on the trailer as the home's foundation.

DIY Considerations

As stated previously, if you are going to do the project yourself, you need to have some knowledge under your belt. Typically, you're going to want to know more than just setting up the frame, interior walls, exterior siding, and roofing. You will also to know about plumbing, power, and other utilities if you want to completely build your tiny house by yourself. If you do not have the know-how knowledge for these utilities, then you may need to hire it out. Most tiny house builders do 50 percent of the work, meaning the framing, roofing, siding, interior walls, flooring, and cabinetry, and let the other 50% be completed by other specialists.

You always want to compare and contrast bids, prices, and building the entire thing on your own. If you have friends with the necessary skills, consider asking them to help you build your home for beer and free lunches. Your friend may also need a project completed that you have the skills for.

One other consideration if you are going to do it yourself, is to consider approaching a design school. If you are not an architect or engineer, find a student who would be willing to get a little cash, as well as extra credit in their course work. The professor can have a final examination of the project to ensure all is legal.

Identifying Criteria and Tiny Home Features

Part of the design, for your home, is going to depend on the criteria you have for your home. What features do you want your home to have? For example, do you want a lot of natural light? Do you want a deck? You have to consider what you want your tiny home to look like, as well as the building materials you want your home to be built with.

Materials Needed for the Construction

Getting recycled materials for the construction of your home is a great option. Recycled materials such as barn wood and other used wood are available for a much lower cost than you'd find in the lumber store. Habitat for Humanity Restores is just one place you can get recycled materials. These restores are filled with items removed from houses that could be used again, such as siding, flooring, plywood, trim, and lathe. At a lower cost than the lumber companies, you can reduce your expenses and still get your required materials.

Wood pallets are another way to get recycled wood for cheap. If you know someone with a lumber or hardware store or even your workplace, you can ask for the pallets without paying anything. Most pallets are going to be destroyed anyway and are simply taking up space at someone's store. The wood can be used for exterior or interior wall coverings versus plywood and drywall.

You can also find doors, cabinets, windows, lights and hardware at recycled material stores like Restores. You could find nearly everything you need to build your tiny house at Restores or through connections. Perhaps, you have a friend that has an old barn that is in need of being taken down. For the labor of taking the structure down, you could ask for the wood to build your tiny house. These types of deals are everywhere—you just have to look for these opportunities.

Concrete, while not recyclable, is also a way to save on certain areas in your home, such as the countertops. Concrete countertops are becoming popular because you can pour the countertops, mix in some coloring, and have a nice smooth counter that will not chip or split.

Countertop materials are also recycled at various stores like Restores, secondhand shops, and antique locations. These counters are usually in great condition, so they can be used again.

Nothing is accepted at these types of stores unless it can be reused.

Windows

Windows are one of the major considerations you need to make. Windows, if not energy efficient, can cost you a lot of solar energy or propane. There are numerous types of windows. Typical frames are made from the following materials:

- Aluminum/Metal
- Composite
- Vinyl
- Wood
- Fiberglass

Vinyl windows are often the most inexpensive windows and have high energy efficiency. The upkeep of vinyl is also less than wood and metal. Unfortunately, the color choices for vinyl are fairly limited.

Wood frames need more upkeep, as well as repainting.

Aluminum and metal frames conduct heat which makes the interior of your home hotter.

Composite and fiberglass windows are a great new option in recent years. However, their costs are higher than vinyl for about the same energy efficiency. The nice thing about composite and fiberglass is that you may be able to find more color options.

You also need to consider the window itself, its glazing or glass. Gas fills provide an insulated glazing, with an improved thermal performance, thus a higher resistance to the heat flow than air fills. There are heat-absorbing tints too, which can reduce the amount of heat transmitted into your home. Insulated windows are best for colder or warmer areas, as a way to keep the temperature neutral in your home. Reflective coatings reduce glare and block more light than they do heat.

For tiny houses, it's recommended to go with low-cost vinyl and ensure it has insulation, such as a double pane, to keep the temperatures neutral. You have a variety of options when it comes to styles.

There are round, square, rectangular, and triangular windows. The more design a window has, the more it is going to cost. The design of your home is also going to determine how many windows you need.

For example, if you want as much wall space as possible, you are going to limit the windows in your wall but need to put several windows where the walls meet your roof. Many people go for a half roof, with a slant, so they can build up one wall to be higher, with a row of rectangular windows for light.

You also have the option of using some of your roof space for skylights, but this can cut down on the solar panels. It is a tradeoff and one you definitely need to consider.

Another choice is to go with a sliding glass door or lanai style door for half your living room. This allows a lot of light in, brings the outside in, and reduces the need for several windows sporadically placed or in the roof.

If you do not want one side of your home to be the door, you could build your front door in the back of your tiny house. The entire back wall could be a sliding glass door, extending 8 feet wide. This could provide you plenty of light, and give you small windows, such as the one over your kitchen sink.

It's also recommended to have a window in the bathroom, to allow heat and moisture to escape post showers.

Brainstorming Utilities for your Tiny House

Utilities include plumbing, heating, air, and electricity. In a tiny house, you need to be particularly careful with what you choose to do include because of the limited space.

Plumbing

You are going to need a bathroom and kitchen. In your kitchen, you are going to need a sink, which has running water. Your bathroom will at least have a shower and sink. These three areas will require plumbing and you do not want to lose interior space due to interior walls. Some people go with traditional plumbing methods, including PVC and copper piping for their tiny houses. In recent years a better alternative to PVC pipes has been used for tiny house plumbing.

PEX tubing is the newest plumbing concept and is better than traditional PVC and copper. PEX is cheaper and much easier to use in confined spaces. It is half an inch thick and bendable. You can't have a kink in it, but you don't need junctions to get the tubing going the way you want it to. You won't need to weld copper pieces and joints together. PEX is also faster to install. It is like running a garden hose from your water unit to the gray water system. The connections you make are a lot quicker than copper since you won't need to solder them together. PEX is also not corrosive like copper, ensuring it holds up better against water particles that tend to corrode copper over time.

PVC and PEX are relatively the same cost. However, PVC requires glue around the joints and PEX doesn't. You can use PEX in vertical and horizontal spaces throughout your tiny house. Unlike PVC plumbing, you don't need a well-ventilated system for PEX. PVC can also freeze and burst. PEX has no such flaws.

For tiny house plumbing, it's recommended to keep your plumbing lines in the interior walls versus exterior walls to prevent freezing.

Although PVC has its flaws, it's not eliminated completely and is still useful for some plumbing of the tiny house. If you are going to have a regular toilet, versus a composite or incinerating toilet then you still need some PVC for waste. Your shower will also need a PVC line running to the gray water. This just ensures that nothing is backed up in the pipe like long hair versus clogging the ½ inch tubing of the PEX. However, PEX can be used for the running water from the water system to the shower, toilet, and sinks.

Bathrooms

The bathroom design in your tiny house is going to be smaller than the average home. There are two common options: a wet bath or using a specialized toilet to avoid waste removal. A wet bath is one where the toilet, sink, floor, and the entire bathroom can get wet. It allows you to combine everything into one room, without a shower curtain. It also makes the shower a lot bigger than closing it off. It requires tile or specialized metal walls.

A tub is an option that most tiny house users opt out of simply because it takes up too much space. However, wine barrels, round tubs, and water troughs have been used, by cutting out the flooring, sinking the tub to floor level, and covering it with a special lid for showing.

Kitchen Sink

Most tiny house users go with a small kitchen sink, without a garbage disposal. However, you can choose a double sink and cover half of it with a cutting board to make more counter space. This offers you an easier time for doing dishes. Most tiny houses avoid having a dishwasher in favor of other appliances and more cabinet space.

Washer/Dryer

Plumbing may also need to include a washer/dryer. There are combo units that will wash and dry. If you want laundry machines in your home, you definitely want the combo unit to save space. This means a running a line to the washer, so you get your clothing clean.

Heating

As you design your tiny house, you need to determine your heating source for the colder months of the year. Most mobile tiny houses do not have space for a wood burning stove. Users also feel they can have a fire outside, versus taking up space with a wood burning stove, but they do like having a "fire" inside the house too. There are ways to get this, including wall inserts and special TV stands that have heaters with fake fire.

Most tiny house owners want to save space, so they limit their heating source to just one. One heating source is usually enough, as long as it's powerful enough to heat the entire structure, even the separate rooms you may have.

You will need to determine how powerful your heater needs to be based on BTUs (British Thermal Unit). Determine the BTUs your heater needs to have by using online calculators. The calculators will ask you the width, length, and the height of your home. It will also ask about the insulating condition. If you have few windows and better than average insulation, then the number of BTUs required to heat your house will be lower. Recall that a standard tiny house is roughly 20 feet in length, by 8 feet in width, by 13 feet high. Let's say hypothetically that a tiny house has normal insulation and the average temperature was 35 degrees Fahrenheit. For this house, 12,432 BTUs or 3,643 watts per hour are needed for your heater. This is about half the BTUs needed for a 1,000 square foot home.

Once you know the size of the heater you need, you can start shopping around. You have options that do not include a large wood stove or central heating. Both would provide too much heat, as well as take up too much space. Instead, there are little furnaces that you can get.

These furnaces are about the size of a hardcover book in height and 4 to 6 inches in width. They do need a pipe, however, which can take up space. The most popular brand of this heater type is Dickinson Marine or Napoleon. Both are wall stoves, which require pipe. If you are going to have a TV, then consider one of the fan powered fake fireplace stands. It won't take up too much space for a small TV, but it will produce the right amount of heat.

Envi heaters are another option. They are wall heaters, but they take up 1/3 of the space of your normal wall heater and run on electricity. If you go with an Envi and live in the mountains, you will need a unit for each room you have, depending on your home design, such as the bathroom and living/bedroom space.

If you plan on traveling to various places, including warm weather locations, you may need a heating and air unit made for tiny houses.

Air Conditioning

If you plan on going to places like Florida, Texas, or living in these areas year round, then you are going to need air conditioning versus heat. Like heaters, the energy efficiency of a unit is paramount to ensuring proper cooling in your home. Window air conditioners are best because they can be placed in the window, without taking up space on the floor or in a room. However, you do lose window light with these units.

A lot of tiny house owners prefer a different method. They like to have more windows, which open. They leave all the windows open when traveling down the road. They also have large doors that open to the outside, setting up the windows and door to provide a cross breeze, and thus ventilation. A ceiling fan can ensure the hot air is stirred up and sent out the windows as the breezes blow. This eliminates the need for air conditioning.

Also, if you are going to be mobile and travel, then you can choose warm locations in winter and cool locations in summer to eliminate the need for air conditioning, and less heat.

Electricity

Electricity is best from solar panels and is the best bang for your buck.

Alternatives, such as propane, can run out and be expensive. It also takes a lot to keep your home regulated. You may not be able to get the right size tank for your needs. Electricity, from an energy source, would require an outside hookup like an RV and a place you could always plug in. It is more trouble than it is worth when traveling since solar power exists.

If you are in a stationary tiny house, then you could use regular power, but this tends to leave a larger carbon footprint, which most tiny house owners prefer to stay away from.

Solar panels run off of batteries, so you will need a battery bank, but the sun will keep those batteries full. When you use electricity, the sun will power your batteries back up. During the day, unless it is gray and cloudy, you can use natural light and very little energy. The batteries are mostly used up at night. Also, consider, using your washer/dryer, and other appliances during the day, when the light is replacing the energy.

Here is what you need to do to determine the amount of electricity you will use and thus the size of solar panels to install.

- Write a list of appliances you want to have in your tiny home: coffee maker, washer/dryer, dishwasher, stove top, oven, etc. Do not forget any of the small appliances such as a toaster, microwave, and mixer. Also, don't forget to list the fridge/freezer.

- On your list, write out how often you use them and for how long. You need to do this for a week.

- You may need to convert the energy use from amps or watts to kilowatt hours.

- As soon as you know the usage of each appliance you will have in your tiny house, you can calculate the number of solar panels and batteries you will need for the system.

- You will need to tell the manufacturer about the conditions your solar panels will go through, such as wind, amount of light, cloud cover, etc.

Your details can vary greatly based on the area you live in. You definitely want to speak with a representative over the phone or in person to get the best results. Online sources can be difficult to get the best rate because there are so many questions a dealer will need to ask.

Your other option is to forgo electricity altogether. If you do this, you will need a wood stove. You will also need camping equipment to make your meals.

Fresh Water Supply

A little was mentioned about the fresh water supply before, but now let's consider your options.

You can collect rainwater by installing a rainwater system. However, if you are in a dry area, then you still need to have a water reservoir.

If you are going mobile, then you will need to stop at places that offer fresh water supplies. Truck stops like Love, Flying J, and other brands have fresh water hookups, where you can fill your tank and empty your gray water. RV sites and some rest stops will have fresh water fill up stations.

This water is going to be cold when you get it from a fill-up location. You are going to need some way to heat it, even if it is rainwater. You do not have to have a huge water heater taking up all your space. There are tankless water heaters that are great, even for regular sized homes. You will want to get a tankless water heater to match your water needs. Most of these do work from propane or electricity, so shop around to choose the most efficient option based on how you are setting up your energy system. This may need to be added into your solar panel calculation.

There are also smaller tank type water heaters designed for RVs. However, they are going to take up more space than if you used a tankless system.

Creating a Functional Kitchen

Kitchens need to be functional. If you cook a lot, consider going for a Nuwave instead of a traditional oven. If not, think about choosing a half stove with 2 burners and an oven that is half the size of a traditional oven.

Additionally, consider the types of cabinets you would want for maximum storage. You could use a corner with rollout storage options. With rollout shelves, you can store things easily in a corner, as well as in front of that storage space. Bigger items can go in the corner. A custom built kitchen for better efficiency is often better than buying pre-made cabinets. Such creative designs may also have an effect on the timeline of your tiny house build, so make sure you have a kitchen concept before you start piecing together your tiny house.

Your Building Timeline

You have ideas for your tiny house. You have explored whether you are going to build it or have someone else do it for you. You have a budget and know what it will take to get materials, electricity, plumbing, heating/air, and fresh water for your tiny house project. Now you just need to determine how long you have to wait until you start living tiny.

If you have a small budget and need to work towards building in stages to cover the costs, then you may take a half year or a few years to get your tiny house built. The magnitude of your commitment for your tiny house project will also contribute to the building timeline.

It's ideal to have a goal, an end date, to make sure your home is built. If you do not have a deadline goal, then you may never get your home built or completed.

If you hire the work done, your contractor will determine much of the timeline based on your budget. They will also hire subcontractors, which also effects building time.

Chapter 4

20 Space Hacks for Living Big in Your Tiny House

Living tiny requires a few tricks to ensure you are as comfortable as possible in your tiny house. The items you want to have, as well as anyone you are bringing with you, are things you must consider.

Pets take up space. They require a place to go to the bathroom, eat, and play. If you have a dog, then you know your dog will be outside going to the bathroom, but for cats, you definitely need a place for the litter box.

What about the washing machine, dishwasher, and other appliances you want? Do you have a collection of something like 400 books and 4 or more tea sets? What are you going to have to leave behind or sell because there is not enough space? The tricks in this chapter are going to help you determine what is possible.

1) **Vertical Spacing**: This is not a new concept, but it has certainly become a lot more important in the last few years. The vertical spacing allows you to use every inch of space you have, going up the walls. If you want to have a hydroponic system for growing lettuce and other vegetables, then you can attach one in your kitchen, using the vertical wall space. Whether you create shelves, nooks, crannies, or wall space for pictures, you can use everything that is not a window.

2) **Multi-storage/purpose furniture** allows you to create storage space, while also using the furniture for other

purposes. There are three different options for multi-storage furniture:

    a. Couches are a great bed, as well as a storage area. The right couch can be a full mattress, without the uncomfortable feeling of a futon. You can also store items underneath the couch, like blankets, games, and clothing. This can be done with drawers or cubbies.

    b. Tables that are built–in can be used as an office, dining table, and game table. They can also be built to encompass multiple seats. An example of a tiny house owner being creative in his design was having a table that folded up into a wall, where the chairs also folded into the wall. One tiny house inventor created a foldable table that had the TV underneath. Another person created stackable chairs that also worked as storage for everyday items.

    c. Pull out baskets built into furniture, stairs, and walls are also multi-purpose. Footstools that are baskets can be used as storage areas. There are also chairs that form one complete unit that has storage inside. They stack together, but the bottom chair has storage too.

    d. Consider vacuum sealed bags for storage in couches or underneath beds. These bags help you eliminate the need for more space and store items not in use each day, like blankets.

3) **Hanging storage space** like baskets is another way for you to get your items where they need to go. Hanging baskets with plants, clothing, dishes, fruit, and much more can be placed on the high ceiling out of your sightline, but provide you with a way to store items.

a. The higher the hanging options the better, so you can use the ceiling space too. For example, bike hangers allow you to store your bikes overhead. You could have a table that uses a winch system, where the table is stored overhead and out of the way.

b. Kitchen utensils can be placed in baskets or buckets that are hung up.

c. You could even have a clothing line that is run in your house, to hang your drying clothing.

d. Ikea is a great place to get hanging storage ideas, whether you are using shoe containers or other items.

4) **Wall mounted beds** like Murphy beds are great in tiny houses. These beds fold up and can save you head space when you are inside. There are twin and larger sizes. If you have young children, wall mounted twin sized beds on top of each other offers a place to sleep. When the children are awake, the beds can make a desk. You can also have a wall mounted bed that turns into your office.

a. Murphy beds are still the most popular, but there are other wall mounted beds as well.

b. Consider including a desk or other feature, such as a TV on the backside of your bed.

c. If wall mounted does not work, think about a slide out bed that is built underneath the flooring to slide out at night.

d. You also have couch conversion options.

5) **Under the staircase storage** provides you with numerous nooks. Staircase storage can be used for clothing, cleaning items, and the smaller nooks can house cat litter boxes, books, shoes, wine, or anything else small that you need to store. People have been pretty inventive with under staircase storage from the roll out counters and desks to sewing storage.

6) **Loft space** is often essential when you only have vertical space to spread work with. A nook or nest on the second floor can be an office, reading area, or your bedroom. If you use it for a bedroom, consider sinking the mattress to be flush with the floor, so you have extra head space. You can also use the floor space as storage, using built in areas between the floor supports, with lift up floorboards. Even the walls in your loft space can become storage. Some innovative individuals have created cat space, by using the walls for little catwalks.

7) Go **Digital and Paperless** because nothing is better than ensuring you have less junk and filing to do in your tiny house. You are not going to have a lot of space for your bills and other mail laying around. You want to keep your space free of unnecessary items, so you have only what you truly want in your home.

8) **Hidden storage** is a perfect way to hide things you don't want to see, like–trash cans. Why have a trash can in an open space? A little nook underneath your sink or in a little hide-a-hole is far better than a trash can where you and others can see it. If you haven't thought of various ways to hide things, then you might wish to seek a little help. For example, if you are using your counter, you could have a draw with a roll out board. A hole the size of your soup pot could be made in it. You have cutting space, but also a place to put the veggies and other items you are cutting up. A fold out counter is another option.

9) **Sliding doors, cabinets, and drawers** can give you more workspace when you need it.

a. You won't have to contend with a pull out that might get in your way or have to be closed for someone else to walk by. However, you may also want some pull outs to extend for more workspace.

b. A combination of both certainly helps you gain more interior space.

c. Barn doors for your bathroom tend to work better than pocket doors or swinging doors. Barn doors slide in and out, without the difficult pocket door contraption. As for swinging doors, they can get in the way.

10) Use **mirrors** in your tiny house. A mirror is not just a bathroom accessory so you can primp. Mirrors help make your space look bigger. The reflection of the mirror ensures you feel your home is much larger than it appears.

11) Tiny houses also need **light tones**. Going with dark walls, furniture, cabinets, and anything else dark, will make your home feel smaller, even smaller than it is. Lighter tones create a great illusion of spaciousness.

12) Plenty of **natural light and fixtures** in your home will also help brighten the space.

a. A lanai or sliding glass door on one wall helps you see better, use less electricity during the day, but also makes your home feel more open and bigger.

b. Using reflective surfaces, not just mirrors, but Plexiglas, metal countertops, and other items can also help lighten a room and make it feel larger.

13) **Pantry shelves** instead of a small room are also better. Yes, it is nice to have a walk in pantry, but living small typically doesn't allow for this. If you do make room for a pantry room, then chances are you're sacrificing valuable space. A small room, without shelves, also adds a mess to deal with. Alternatively, figure out ways you can eat fresh foods that are healthier that allow you to limit your pantry storage.

Pantry shelves can help you organize what you do have and save you tons of space. Consider getting adjustable pantry shelves to fit the items you are going to buy at any given time.

14) Use your **outside space** too. Some people have built decks that latch up and cover their sliding glass door. These decks are built with pulleys or winches. They go up when the tiny house is in movement and come down when the mobile tiny house is stationary.

15) **Grills** are possible. A deck can provide you with great outdoor space, which can also be a place to have a built in grill. You can also have it roll out from the inside to the outside with your grill. Another grill option is to build it to come up from the frame of the trailer.

16) If you have a **neck** on your trailer, where you build your bedroom, the underneath area can be storage for plenty of things like bikes, scuba gear, generators, air compressors, propane, mechanic tools, and much more. This space can literally be anything you wish it to be.

17) Start watching **tiny house shows**, there are even tiny house TV shows now. These shows provide you with innovations you might not have considered. Some storage options have been mentioned thus far, but it's not until you see them visually, that you start putting pieces together to incorporate in your own tiny house, for example, a moveable roof or walls.

   a. Did you know it was possible to use a pulley system to increase your ceiling height? You could also use winches. While you are restricted to 13 feet when on the road, you can have a roof that is built over the exterior of your 8-foot 6-inch width or built to go inside that space. It takes some innovation, but it can be done.

   b. You can also have moveable walls that are on winches, powered by electricity or require two people to expand. These walls provide more floor space and seating than when it is closed. For instance, you could have a section that moves out 4 feet on one side and 4 feet on the other. When open you have walking space and seating. When closed you have a full sized bed.

18) **Utilizing the floor** is another option. One owner wanted to have a controlled wine area in his tiny house. There was a wine cooler built into the floor of the kitchen, which could be opened by pulling up and extracting the wine. The floor feature was built in between the trailer and the floor that was raised up to account for the wheel wells of the trailer. You could turn the floor into a bookshelf covered in Plexiglas. It could be a storage area for clothing or other flat items as well.

19) Stationary tiny homes can be built out of **wood or shipping containers**. If you want to live small, but save on costs, consider starting with a shipping container for framing. You would need a welder to cut in windows, but the doors could be used to open up your container. You could also have a slider built in for the main door. Shipping container homes can be pieced together for more area too. They can also be stacked if you want to have multiple levels.

20) **Roofs** can be made into decks, living roofs, or used for your solar panels. A living roof, means you have plants growing on there for edible and medicinal uses. In fact, a lot of ways to save on space is to start growing what you are going to eat and use for medicinal purposes. The reason for this is because you don't need a large pantry, you don't need a place for medicines, and you can always eat what you are growing.

Chapter 5

Frequently Asked Questions

Tiny house enthusiasts looking to start their project have plenty of questions about what they need to do to get their home built and become livable.

Is living in a tiny house for everyone?

No, you truly need to know yourself to determine if you can live tiny and how tiny will be comfortable for you. A question you should ask yourself is can you share less than 400 square feet with someone else, without feeling claustrophobic? Second, can you store things appropriately? If you are disorganized, claustrophobic, or need a lot of floor space—tiny house living may not be for you. Tiny house owners are perceived to be hyper-organized to live tiny, generally because they're forced to be due to the limited space.

Other things to take into account are tiny house habits that you'll pick up. Your bed may need to be put away every day. You have to do the dishes each day. Living also requires you to be a minimalist because you can't buy numerous things and hope to store them in your tiny home. Your space is too limited.

Should I have a staircase or a ladder to get to the second floor of my tiny house?

If you have a second floor, then you are going to need to decide the best way to get to that floor. There are innovative methods you can implement to get upstairs. Two common ways are having a staircase or using a ladder.

Ladders are most typical because you can place them against a wall, when not in use and make them hide or you can go with a straight up and down option that takes up less space.

Staircases, when built in a normal fashion, take up space, but also give you storage. A staircase can become a closet for clothing, washer/dryer, books, or even a dinner table, chairs, or a desk. Another concept is to use a winch and a swing. You can have the winch pull you to the ceiling and swing to your second floor.

It all depends on whether you need storage space or more floor space.

What are common obstacles in the tiny house creation process?

The top three are:

- Height/width/length
- Storage
- Eliminating items, you don't need

The size hinders you and ensures you to truly think about what you want in your home and what is most important. Storage requires you to eliminate a lot of things you have collected.

How can I find tiny house communities near me?

Research is the best way and in the digital age, it's much easier than ever before. There are currently communities in Boulder, Colorado; Lyons, Colorado; and Portland, Oregon. Many RV locations also allow tiny houses, but they are more of an RV community versus tiny house community. Washington state has a couple locations around Seattle and on the peninsula. Port Townsend is definitely a static tiny house community, as well as an artist colony.

Do the advantages of tiny house living outweigh the disadvantages?

This is a subjective question and has no true answer. You have to determine if the advantages of a tiny house are going to outweigh the things you lose in a larger home. Only you can determine if you can live tiny.

Is going solar the best option for my utilities in my tiny house?

Yes, because the sun will generate your power. You won't need an electrical hookup or to spend a lot on filling your small propane tank. You can start with a propane tank, but solar panels are something to shoot for down the road.

Can I have a microwave in my tiny house?

Yes; however, you will have a decision to make. Microwaves take up a lot of counter space or under the cabinet space. If you are not going to use a real stove to make meals, then you could probably go with buying frozen dinners and living with a microwave.

Stoves and ovens take up a lot of space and things can quickly become cluttered with a microwave. A combination could be a NuWave, which can be stored, but used to heat up food as well as prepare it. You can also just go with a real stove for heating up food. If a microwave is a must then shop for the smallest one you can get.

What else can I do to heat up my tiny house during cold weather?

If you have an oven and washer/dryer combination, use these appliances when you are home. If necessary, have a small camping stove that you can use in the room where you are present.

Radiant heated floors are definitely a great option to help increase the heat in your home. Radiant heat is made in thermal panels or cord like the PEX plumbing, only thinner. You can attach it under your flooring and hook it to your electricity. It's a great design strategy for adding a secondary heat source in your tiny house.

Should I have a PO Box?

If you are going mobile, then you need to have a place to get your mail. A PO box will not interfere with friends or relatives mail. It also ensures your mail is delivered someplace when you make a stop. For those who go off the grid, a PO box also provides anonymity.

Should my roof be flat?

There are a few reasons to have a flat roof. Weather can cause leaks in a flat roof; however, certain tiny home designers have gone flat to create a deck overhead. It takes more work to ensure the roof is completely sealed. A flat roof can offer you a more abundant bedroom nook, office, and more lighting.

On the other hand, sloped roofs can make your home appear larger inside than it truly is.

What's the best roofing material?

Recycled metal is best for roofing material. It is a little more expensive than 30-year shingles, but it will last a lifetime. Plus, you can still secure your solar panels to the roof. If you live in cold weather places, the metal will conduct heat, helping keep your interior warmer.

Can I recycle my water usage?

There are ways to reuse your water. You would need a more expensive gray water system with a filtration system. It would need to have chemicals added and go through a cleaning process before it could be used again. However, it is possible.

How do I keep my plumbing pipes from freezing in the winter?

The best thing to do is have them inside the floor, with added insulation, as well as running them through an inside wall. If you need to put pipes on the outside wall, consider wrapping the pipes with insulation manufactured for plumbing. Also, leave your cabinet doors open in the cooler temperatures, so heat reaches the pipes.

Can I put a laundry machine in my tiny house?

Yes, there will be more electricity and space demand. A combo unit is going to work best to keep usage to a minimum—not to mention saving space.

What do most tiny house users do about bathroom concerns and showering?

Most tiny house users go for composite toilets, a small pedestal sink, and a 3 by 3 shower.

Is it best to hire contractors and professionals for a tiny house project?

Your experience determines how beneficial it is to hire experts. Experts are beneficial for most tiny house owners because they know zoning laws and engineering concepts that make it possible to build a great and safe home.

Can I park my tiny house anywhere?

There are open road laws. Boondocking is an option like it is with RVing. Boondocking means you can park on "free land," usually national park land. Any land that has a do not trespass sign on it, should not be used, unless you have inquired with the owners. You can park on your friend's or family's land if they allow it. Most of the time you will need to park in tiny house communities, RV locations, or campgrounds. You can also park at truck stops if they allow you to. However, each truck stop is different, so you will need to ask when you see one, if you wish to stop at and park overnight. Typically, you have to pay for parking like an RV at most locations.

Where should I build my tiny house?

There are expert builders in Colorado, Oregon, Washington, Tennessee, and Arkansas. There are also a few sporadic experts in places like Wisconsin, Michigan, and Pennsylvania. The best place to build is where you live or where the experts are located near. If you are going with a stationary tiny house, then anywhere you want to live is fine.

Can I have a TV?

Yes, you can have a TV. Unless you are parking somewhere that offers cable hookups, you are going to need to invest in satellite service. Compare Dish and DIRECTV to determine the best costs.

Can I still use the internet?

You will need to conduct research; however, you can establish a mobile hotspot. There are several ways to do this. Your mobile phone company offers you a mobile hotspot option, where you pay for a dongle that plugs into your computer. You pay for a certain amount of gigabytes usage in a month. If you depend on your internet for TV, as well as work, then you may need to create a mobile access point, which might have to be a satellite. Satellites ensure that you have the internet anywhere there is a sightline to the sky. As you move across the country, you would need to tap into different satellites, making sure there is always a clear view of the sky. Keep in mind that rain and inclement weather can greatly interfere with satellite internet.

Most mobile phone companies are developing more affordable options, so do research to find the best one for you. You will also need to know how much internet you actually use in a month's time to save on options.

Conclusion

I hope this book was able to help you with your tiny house needs and questions.

The next step is to start planning out your tiny house. You will want to layout square footage maps on your floor with tape or other items. You should determine if you can live and move into a tiny space.

Consider renting a tiny house that is the same size you are considering building. This way, you test whether you can truly live in such a home. It should be for a month, not just a week. Most anything can be will—powered for a week.

Once you know you can live in a tiny house for a week, it is time to work on the heating, appliances, and overall design. The design planning may take a physical layout of your floor space, paper, using a computer, or a mixture. Be sure to speak with experts about the limitations you may face in building the tiny house based on your needs.

Thank you and good luck!

Resources

Tiny House consulting: www.tinyhousecraftsman.com

Tiny House floor plan designs:

www.thesmallhousecatalog.com

http://www.thetinyhouse.net/skip-the-trailer-13-tiny-

houses-built-on-foundations/

Forums:

http://www.livingbiginatinyhouse.com/tiny-house-

forums/

http://tinyhouseforums.com/

Community Living Discovery:

http://tinyhousecommunity.com/forums.htm

Made in the USA
Middletown, DE
20 November 2016